Red Ladder Theatre Company proudly presents

T0316237

WHERE'S VIETNAM?

Written by Alice Nutter

Directed by Rod Dixon

First performed at the Courtyard Theatre, West Yorkshire Playhouse, Leeds
19-21 June 2008

Cast

Indra J Adler	Mary / Student
Hayley Avron	Student
Tanja Bage	Jennifer
Regan Bevons	Wife / Student
Hannah Briggs	Rox / Student
Sophie Carter	Student
Ellen Chivers	Cake Lady / Violinist / Student
Carolyn Eden	Rox / Student
Leah Francis	Celie
John Geoghegan	Student / Policeman
Peter Gordon	Richard / Cop / Student
David Graham	Driver / Student / Cop
John Guilor	Top Cop / Student
Christopher Haigh	Carl / Student
Ella Harris	Treefrog
Catherine Holden	Rox / Student
Kus Mandela	Moz
Robert McLaughlan	Vicar / Student / Cop
Bryan Outlaw	Cop / Student
Rachel Rudd	Wife / Student
Samantha Richardson	Student
Gerard Savva	Jethro / Student / Cop
Rakhee Kumari Sharma	Student
Ian Sharpe	Cop / Student
Paul Simmons	Driver / Student / Cop
Carla Starkey	Rox / Student
Warwick St John	Richard / Cop / Student
David Toole	Banks
Mike White	Jethro / Student / Cop
David Zezulka	Arthur

The Nam Band

Richard Bostock	Sax
Alex Dale	Bass
Jem Dobbs	Trumpet
Jonny Flockton	Guitar
Adam Smith	Keyboard
Jacqui Wicks	Vocals

Creative Team

Written by	Alice Nutter
Director	Rod Dixon
Assistant Director	Justin Audibert
Set & Costume Designer	Ali Allen
Set Design Assistant	Uzma Kazi
Assistant Designer/Set & Prop Maker	Charlotte Stanley
Costumes	Becky Graham
Composer & Musical Director	Harry Hamer
Sound Designer	Jaydev Mistry
Choreographer	Sharon Watson
Lighting Designer	Tim Skelly / Tim Thornally
Stage Manager	Calum Clark
Set Builders	Q Division / Marcus Rapley

Red Ladder Management Team

Chris Lloyd	General Manager
Stefanie Gascoigne	Tour Manager
Laura Hamlet	Assistant Administrator
Dan Jeffrey	Press & PR

Thank you to:

Arts Council of Yorkshire & England for your continuing belief and support of our work, and the staff at West Yorkshire Playhouse for the opportunity to create and share our work with you.

Biographies

Alice Nutter   Writer

Alice Nutter was formerly a lyricist and long-serving member of the anarchist pop band Chumbawamba before hanging the mic up at the end of 2004 to concentrate on writing drama. While a member of the band Alice had a stint as a journalist and Features Editor at the now defunct *Leeds Other Paper/ Northern Star*.

Alice has also been a lyric writer on film scores including Alex Cox's *Revenger's Tragedy* and *Stigmata*.

Originally from Burnley, Alice now lives in Leeds and describes herself as a writer who ended up in a band. She recently wrote Episode 5, 'The Postman', for Jimmy McGovern's BAFTA-winning TV series *The Street*.

Rod Dixon   Director

Rod grew up in the culturally diverse city of Liverpool. He became Director of Red Ladder Theatre Company in 2006. Before this, Rod was Associate Director at the Barbican Theatre in Plymouth and as a freelancer directed several shows at Plymouth Theatre Royal. Before running The Hub Theatre School in Cornwall, Rod had been an actor with several companies including Kneehigh Theatre.

Since being with Red Ladder Rod has directed two national touring shows (*Kaahini* by Maya Chowdhry re-tour 2006 and *Doors* by Madani Younis 2007), developed The Red Grit Young Actors Training Company and forged International links with a Palestinian Theatre Company, Al Harah Theatre who are based in Beit Jala, a small town near Bethlehem in the West Bank. The aim of this relationship is to eventually lead to a co-production, which will tour the UK and Middle East. Watch this space...

Justin Audibert   Assistant director

Justin is currently Assistant Director in residence at the West Yorkshire Playhouse and is studying for the Arts Council MFA in Theatre Directing at Birkbeck College, London.

For the West Yorkshire Playhouse, Justin has been Assistant Director on *Fast Labour* (Hampstead Theatre), *The Grouch*, *Runaway Diamonds* (WYP Touring) and the Christmas hit *Beauty and the Beast,* as well as Told By An Idiot's *Casanova* (UK Tour, Lyric Hammersmith) and Justin has directed two short plays, *Ready Mades* and *Trinity's Saint* as part of Leeds Light Night '07.

Before coming to Leeds he assisted Richard Beecham on *A Month in the Country* and Nick Tudor on *Nana*, both at ArtsEd, London and also assisted Ken Christiansen (Operating Theatre Company) on *A Torture Comedy* (Tristan Bates Theatre).

Future directing work includes co-directing an original piece of music theatre; *Armley: The Musical*, by Boff Whalley, this July and also directing the premiere of *Company Along the Mile*, by Tom Dalton Bidwell at the West Yorkshire Playhouse in January 2009.

Ali Allen Designer

Ali was born in Somerset and studied Fine Art at Newcastle University; she has been based in Leeds for 28 years.

Ali's work has extended over a wide variety of areas including carnival, sculpture, pantomime, opera and outdoor theatre projects. Carnival work has taken her to Trinidad where she and Marise Rose won best float in 1996, and to Brooklyn for Labour Day parade in 1997.

Ali has designed many touring sets for companies such as Major Road, Pilot Theatre and Red Ladder, for whom she has designed around six sets.

Other theatre credits include *Rumblefish, Bloodtide, The Twits, Fungus the Bogeyman* and the award-winning *Lord of the Flies* for Pilot Theatre, *Kes* and *Brassed off* for Lawrence Batley Theatre, Huddersfield, *Bollywood Jane* for Leicester Haymarket, and *Once Upon a Quarry Hill* for West Yorkshire Playhouse, *Look Back in Anger* for Harrogate Theatre, and *Camel Station* for writer Trevor Griffiths.

Ali also designed *Madame Butterfly, Wuthering Heights* and *Dracula* for Northern Ballet Theatre, and was assistant designer to Peter Mumford on *Peter Pan.*

Sharon Watson
Choreographer

Sharon, a graduate of the London School of Contemporary Dance began her career working with Phoenix Dance Theatre in Leeds under Directors Neville Campbell, Margret Morris and Thea Barnes, over the years both performing and choreographing, as well as taking on the role of Rehearsal and Tour Director.

Sharon's career has included extensive performances by the likes of Philip Taylor, Donald Byrd, Bebe Miller, Tom Jobe, Michael Clarke, Shapiro and Smith, as well as lecturing at the Northern School of Contemporary Dance in Leeds, setting up her own company, Arts Beyond Contemporary Dance, and producing her own work, with her piece *Never Still* being taken to the 1996 Olympics in Atlanta as part of the cultural entertainment.

More recently, Sharon undertook the Cultural Leadership course 2006, which lead her to work for four months at The Sage Gateshead, devising and delivering a dancers and composers course. Adding to her development, in September 2007 Sharon embarked on an MA at the Leeds Metropolitan University in Performance Works, reflecting her deep interest in the creative powers and engaging in debate whilst exploring new ways of working.

Harry Hamer
Musical Director

Harry is a musician, songwriter and composer. His career spans film, the music industry and more recently theatre. He was a performer, composer, producer and all-round member of the pop band Chumbawamba (1983–2004). His work also includes music for Ken Loach (Channel 4), *Revengers Tragedy* by Alex Cox (Avenging Angel Film), *Whatever*, a Teenage Musical by Daisy Asquith (Channel 4) and *Foxes* by Alice Nutter (Northern Exposure).

Other music accolades as producer and musician include Sufferin Succotash, Alabama 3, New Model Army, Oysterband, Jo Freya's Lal Waterson Project and Credit to the Nation. He continues to live in Leeds.

Tim Skelly Lighting

Tim Skelly is a resident theatre designer and academic at the Workshop Theatre, University of Leeds. He has also worked as an academic at University College Bretton Hall in Wakefield and as a resident practitioner and teacher of lighting design at the Royal Academy of Dramatic Art in London.

As a freelance lighting designer recent professional work includes *NHS* and *Union Street* for Plymouth Theatre Royal; *Wars of the Roses* and *Runaway Diamonds* for West Yorkshire Playhouse; *Doors* and *Kaahini* for Red Ladder Theatre Company; *Three Sisters* and *Romeo and Juliet* for Colchester Mercury Theatre; *Chiaroscuro, Playfall, Plunge, Somewhere Inside* and *High Land* for Scottish Dance Theatre; and technical management and lighting support for *Cattlecall*, *Picadores* and *Paseillo* for Phoenix Dance Theatre.

Tim also works as a lighting consultant for *Yorkshire Sculpture Park* and has collaborated with several artists, including lighting designs for Sir Anthony Caro's *The Trojan Wars*, and retrospectives for Philip King and Christo.

In his academic capacity he has won an award from the British Academy Arts and Humanities Research Board to complete a survey of key British Lighting Designers from the late twentieth century.

Calum Clark Stage Manager

Company Stage Manager, Calum Clark, has been making choices since 1971. One of the first being to keep his poor mother and father awake as much as possible with his appalling night time antics, thus resulting in him remaining an only child. With no siblings to encourage rivalry, play with or inspire, he spent a lot of time alone drawing, writing, recording, and forging the beginnings of what was to become a career in THE ARTS. With over fifteen years experience as an artist, designer, performer, director, musician and stage manager, Calum is now encouraging his parents to at least consider adoption.

David Toole (Banks)

Dave Toole was born in and still lives in Leeds; he started a career in the arts after attending a workshop with CandoCo Dance Company in 1992. After touring with them for six years he left to pursue other opportunities and has since worked with many companies including DV8 (*The Cost of Living*) and Graeae Theatre Company (*Blasted*) and most recently with the RSC (*I'll be the Devil*). His film work includes Sally Potter's *The Tango Lesson*, *Outside In* for CandoCo and also *Amazing Grace*.

He has also played numerous small roles in a number of TV and film productions the most recent being that of a mad man announcing the death of Caesar in the second series of *Rome* for HBO.

This is David's second appearance with Red Ladder.

Ella Harris (Treefrog)

Like Treefrog Ella is experimenting. She finished her acting training at the Royal Scottish Academy of Music and Drama in Glasgow in 1994, and has since worked with several professional companies. Until recently she has specialised in improvisational theatre and in 2006 she set up Mirror Mirror Theatre Company, which continues to use stories from the audience to create spontaneous theatre.

She is also a qualified practitioner and trainer in EFT – a 'must have' personal survival tool for the 21st century and born only four years after the Grosvenor Square demo, Ella is busy preparing for the next revolution.

RED LADDER
THEATRE COMPANY

Red Ladder is based at the Yorkshire Dance Centre, Leeds. The company has a national reputation, regularly tours the UK and is funded by Arts Council, Yorkshire.

Red Ladder's mission is to 'make theatre which celebrates, inspires and challenges young people, developing in them the desire and ability to express ideas and strengthen social and cultural cohesion.'

The company, founded in 1968 in London, has a colourful history that spans 40 years, from the radical socialist theatre movement in Britain known as agitprop, to the company's current position. In the 70's the company moved to Leeds, where it is still based today, and during the 80's the company redefined itself, specialising in creating work that targeted specific audiences: Asian; Black; gender specific & deaf groups.

Today the company is acknowledged as one of Britain's leading national touring companies producing high quality new plays for diverse audiences and manages to reinvent itself without losing its fundamental aim of reaching parts other companies don't, won't or can't.

We aim to:

- celebrate and build upon Red Ladder's 40 year history of making theatre.
- include young people in the creative processes of making theatre
- embellish current text-driven practice by experimentation with new theatre practice – including working with other art forms
- inspire a new generation of theatre makers through the quality and originality of our creative practice
- tour this work nationally, targeting young people who have little or no access to theatre
- seek international collaboration actively and to engage with theatre making in troubled parts of the world – helping ordinary people investigate global issues
- create a reputation for a unique Red Ladder artistic process and a 21st-century style – to compliment the reputation that precedes us.
- continue to raise our local and regional profile particularly through enabling and inspiring emerging local artists

Red Ladder Theatre Company
3 St. Peter's Buildings, York Street, Leeds LS9 8AJ
Tel: 0113 245 5311
Email: info@redladder.co.uk
www.redladder.co.uk

Director's Notes

1968: I remember sitting with my mum and dad watching the news – black and white telly footage of students and workers marching to protest against the war in Vietnam at the American Embassy in Grosvenor Square. I was shocked; my parents were shocked; they tutted with disgust at 'the long-haired louts' tussling with the police; I was stunned by the police violence on the screen – young women being pulled to the ground by their hair, police truncheons cracking skulls of unarmed protestors…and at ten years old I understood that the right to protest in this country is as fragile as anywhere in the world. I ran out into the street and chalked 'Peace' on the pavement – and got a clout on the back of the head from our next-door neighbour.

Celebrating 40 years of making theatre for the common people, Red Ladder's production of Alice Nutter's new musical, *Where's Vietnam?* is our attempt to clout that neighbour back!!

I am extremely proud to be Artistic Director of Red Ladder. The company has such a long and exciting history and many artists who have worked with the company have gone on to influence the British theatre industry. As an old-fashioned Socialist I still believe that theatre can and should provoke, agitate and move audiences to want to improve their lives and our society. Starting as a street theatre protest in Grosvenor Square in 1968, Red Ladder Theatre Company is still 'out there' raising audiences' awareness of key modern issues. I am very keen to develop a very definite Red Ladder aesthetic, but as can be seen in this production, we are open to playing with a range of styles, and this piece of musical theatre is a first for the company. Finally, I would like to congratulate all the artists and the cast of *Where's Vietnam?* for their very considerable hard work and commitment. The enthusiasm of everyone involved in this production has made it a joy to work on.

Rod Dixon
May 2008

Writer's Notes

When Rod Dixon first approached me and asked me to think about submitting ideas for Red Ladder's 40 anniversary play, I realised that it was an ideal opportunity to write about 1968, the moment when pop and politics merged and the world was in flux. I wanted to explore the effect that conflagration had on ordinary people's lives.

Coming from Burnley, the effects of sexual and political revolution of 1968 took about ten years to filter through. Punk rock opened up the world for me in the late seventies and widened my parameters so I thought I could have an alternative future to working on the checkout at Asda – which I hated.

For me, *Where's Vietnam?* is a chronicle of a moment where working class people could glimpse alternate futures. It's a play about change – and one that's stuffed with music and comedy.

Alice Nutter
May 2008

To
all of the artists who have worked with Red Ladder
past, present and future…

WHERE'S VIETNAM?

Characters

BANKS

ARTHUR

CELIE

MOZ

ROX

JENNIFER

JETHRO

CARL

DRIVER

WOMAN

MARY

RICHARD

TREEFROG

CAKE LADY

HIPPY dressed as VICAR

COFFIN BEARERS

USHERS

TOP COP

BAND, COPS

WORKING CLASS KITCHEN – MORNING

BANKS is sitting in his wheelchair, behind a table. On the table is a cake with five candles on. His brother ARTHUR, a bear of a man, sits reading a Tintin comic. The brothers wear sharp mohair suits, white shirts, thin ties and shiny shoes. BANKS opens a bag and lovingly lays out knuckle dusters, a knife and a small billy club. BANKS picks up the billy club and taps it against his palm.

BANKS pours himself a gin and tonic from bottles on the table.

BANKS: Come on, have one.

ARTHUR: Not had me cornflakes yet. And we're having the cake soon. I'll just have tonic.

BANKS: Tonic… I offer you the Krays' favourite tipple and you ask for a glass of pop.

BANKS pours ARTHUR a gin and tonic.

Get that down you.

Pause.

I know why you bought that cake.

ARTHUR puts his comic down.

ARTHUR: Five years, today's special.

BANKS: You sure you didn't just want a pudding?

ARTHUR lights the candles.

ARTHUR: We have to mark today.

BANKS: Soft, that's your problem, soft.

Pause.

Only thing we have to mark is him.

ARTHUR: Gonna pick him up at the gates?

BANKS: What and give plod a nod while we're there? Five years I've waited for that horny little prick, I can last another few hours. Come on, pick your glass up... Made it Ma, Top of the world!

ARTHUR: (*Clinks glasses.*) Top of the world!

Motions to cake.

Feels like we should sing.

BANKS: Launch into a show tune and I'm off.

Pause.

Come on then, blow.

ARTHUR: You do it. Don't forget to wish.

BANKS blows the candles out.

ARTHUR pulls the candles off the cake and picks up the knife from BANKS' kit and starts to cut the cake.

BANKS: Whoa! That's a handcrafted English patterned bowie.

ARTHUR: (*Eating a huge slice.*) I'll wipe it after.

BANKS: It's an antique, supposedly used in the wild west to scalp Indians, though the rip-off merchant who sold it me was a Grade A fibber. One thing's for certain, it's a killing machine not a cake slice.

ARTHUR: I'll get another knife. Do you want a plate? I could get Mum's china out.

BANKS: Leave it. Not a tea party.

Pause.

It's embarrassing, there'll be doilies next.

ARTHUR: There's only you and me here.

BANKS: Does John Wayne put bows in his horse's mane when no-one's looking?

ARTHUR: No.

BANKS: Does he request his nag call him Marion?

ARTHUR: Horses can't talk, except Mr Ed –

BANKS: That's not a horse it's an actor.

ARTHUR: In a horse's suit?

BANKS: Jesus, sponge your front.

BANKS picks up the knuckle dusters and slips them on.

ARTHUR: Bet he won't be armed.

BANKS: Hence it comes about that all armed Prophets have been victorious, and all unarmed Prophets have been destroyed.

BANKS takes the knuckle dusters off and gets a stiletto knife out of his bag of tricks. He hands it to ARTHUR.

Carry this today.

ARTHUR: I'll use my fists.

BANKS: Put it down your sock.

ARTHUR: Don't want to cut me leg.

BANKS: It's in a case, Einstein.

ARTHUR puts the knife on the table.

BANKS gets a bottle of pills out of his pocket. Takes one with his gin and tonic.

ARTHUR watches disapprovingly.

What are you my physician now?

ARTHUR: Never said anything.

BANKS: If I wanted dirty looks I'd get myself a girlfriend.

PRISON GATES – MORNING

CELIE, 19, waits across from the prison gates. MOZ, 24, comes out of the prison gates wearing a Beatles suit. The door slams behind him. He carries an envelope with his possessions in it. CELIE waves at her brother.

MOZ: So much for the brass band. (*Shouting to CELIE.*) Hang on a minute...

MOZ bends over, pulls his pants down and shows his arse to the prison gate.

My arse your place!

PRISON GUARD: (*Bored, unseen behind grill.*) Nobody's ever done that before.

The grill slams shut.

CELIE rushes over, hugs MOZ quickly. Starts pushing him along.

CELIE: Bus goes in an hour.

MOZ: What bus?

CELIE: Your bus. Birmingham, you're going to Birmingham –

MOZ: Seeing Mum before I go anywhere.

CELIE: Aunty Sheila says you can stay at hers; her lodger's dead.

Grabs MOZ's arm.

C'mon.

MOZ: Thought Mum would be here!

CELIE: She couldn't. –

MOZ: Once, she came to see me, once! –

CELIE: Upset her, when she went to the ladies –

MOZ: There was a sign on the wall, 'Don't piss on the floor your son will have to clean it up', I know...but I'm out now.

CELIE: She's not. Her nerves are terrible, can't even answer the door.

MOZ: Got a present for her.

CELIE: I'll give it her.

MOZ: Been looking forward to a fry up.

CELIE roots in her bag and slaps a butty and a can of pop into his hand.

CELIE: Dairylea, salad cream, dandelion and burdock.

CELIE gets an envelope out.

Eleven pounds, ten shillings and sixpence, tide you over till you're on your feet.

MOZ: Thing is… I've told a mate of mine that I'd stop off at his…

CELIE: You're getting on that bus.

MOZ: C'mon… Aunty Sheila's… I've been inside five years, I'm not going into a nunnery!

CELIE: She's not a nun, she's born again.

MOZ: Last time I saw her she was singing 'The Old Rugged Cross' with a tambourine.

CELIE: Well at least she won't stab you with it.

MOZ: Banks doesn't know I'm out! C'mon, one night out with my clever sister…we've never celebrated you getting into college. I were made up when I got that letter.

Pause.

I'd have done another three months wi'out it. I were cracking up…no baccy and the senile old sod I had to share a cell with wun't stop coughing. If he'd brought up one more greeny, swear I'd have smashed the cell up… then the screws hand me your letter, couldn't believe it, fine art… I thought, in hundreds of years time my sister's paintings are gonna be in Woolworths.

Pause.

That deserves a drink.

CELIE: Thanks. Well have one when I come and visit you. If I have to handcuff you to the seat, you're getting on that bus.

MOZ: (*Stops, pulls really terrible clown watercolour out.*) It's for Mum. Did it in art class…took weeks…the other lads made their Mothers gypsy caravans out of match sticks but Mum always loved that clown on Nan's wall.

CELIE: Looks sad.

She examines it a bit closer.

It says Jonesy, down there, it's signed Jonesy!

MOZ: Okay, I didn't paint it but it did cost me three fags and a comb.

CELIE pulls one out of her handbag. MOZ crosses 'Jonesy' out, spits on his fingers and rubs the corner into a blur. Signs it again. Hands it back to CELIE.

Can go above the bureau.

The noise of traffic takes over. They stop by a bus stop.

Need a pee.

CELIE roots in her bag and hands him an empty bottle.

No way! I've waited five years for a toilet door that locks. First day out and I have to have a slash in a bottle! Not doing it.

MOZ starts to walk away from the bus stop.

I'm going to Mum's.

CELIE: She won't let you in.

MOZ: What?

CELIE: She's ashamed.

MOZ: But she never said –

CELIE: And Dad dropped dead because of you.

MOZ: He smoked sixty a day and…it were a heart attack! –

CELIE: You broke his heart.

Pause.

And Mum's…turning up at the funeral in handcuffs.

MOZ: You think I chose that?

CELIE: You wash back up and it all starts again. It's your fault she's in a state.

Pause.

Do everybody a favour and get on the bus, promise me you'll get on the bus.

MOZ nods.

WORKING CLASS BACKYARD – DAY

ARTHUR is in vest and old fashioned sweat pants skipping. BANKS is zipping around him in circles in his wheel chair.

ARTHUR: It's bugging me, I'm dizzy!

BANKS: Get more bugged.

ARTHUR: Shouldn't have had that gin and tonic.

BANKS: Shouldn't have had the cake. You're a fighter…what are you?

ARTHUR: A fighter.

Pause.

I've got a stitch.

BANKS: Work through it. Can't stop a fight for a stitch.

ARTHUR: Water? Can I have some water?

BANKS: Not yet… C'mon…he's right across from you…get right in his ear…come on say it!

ARTHUR: Do I have to?

BANKS: It's crucial.

ARTHUR: (*Half hearted.*) I've fucked your Mother.

BANKS: And your Grandmother…you're winding him up, throw a few adjectives in.

ARTHUR: Your Mother smells.

BANKS: Jesus, of what, Chanel Number 5? Psychological warfare, think Cassius Clay, the fight starts before you get into the ring. Needle 'em, don't let 'em think straight, knock the stuffing out of 'em without throwing a punch.

ARTHUR: You have to call him Ali now, he dun't like Cassius. (*Does Ali impression.*) 'What's my name fool, what's my name?'

Pause.

It was Muhammed Ali after that fight.

BANKS: See, hit 'em hard enough and you can get anybody to call you anything you want.

Pause.

The Krays know 'em all.

ARTHUR: They know Ali?

BANKS: The British champions. Henry Cooper, they send his Mother a hamper every Christmas.

ARTHUR: I like that tinned ham you get –

BANKS: Concentrate. Come on, float like a butterfly, sting like a bee.

ARTHUR: (*Panting and stopping skipping.*) I've no footwork.

BANKS: Negativity. What have I told you?

ARTHUR: Takes confidence to pull a confidence trick.

BANKS: (*Passes ARTHUR a drink.*) Precisely. You can take punishment you don't need to get out of the way. Get your head down here.

ARTHUR ducks and BANKS gets out a clean white hanky. BANKS tenderly wipes the sweat off ARTHUR's face as he talks, like a trainer cooling down a champion horse.

(*Taps ARTHUR's chest.*) Talent for violence hiding in there… just haven't worked out how to tap into it yet. You're a Banks…look at our Dad, best bare-knuckle fighter in Leeds. It's in the blood.

ARTHUR: If it doesn't work out…

BANKS: Course it'll work out –

ARTHUR: Could take up something else…

BANKS: Like what? You need to be tough in this business.

ARTHUR: Rugby, rugby's tough.

BANKS: If you want a bunch of morons to jump on you, get yourself into town on a Saturday night.

Pause.

You've too much heart for someat that's you against the pack. You'd die trying to stay on your feet. You can dine out on boxing, all you'll eat through rugby is turf. It's all about respect, innit?

ARTHUR: Suppose so.

BANKS: Trick to any transaction is not to deal in the moment, when you're in the ring, toe to toe with a bag of muscle, you're not up against THAT particular fucker –

ARTHUR: Am I up against myself?

BANKS: Where've you got that crap?

ARTHUR: Somebody handed me a pamphlet.

BANKS: And they say literacy's the way forward.

Pause.

Come on, who do you despise?

ARTHUR: Peter Purves. He's on *Blue Peter*.

BANKS: I'm despairing.

ARTHUR: Moz… I hate Moz, you know I hate Moz.

BANKS: At last. Right, every man you have in front of you is Moz, get his mug tattooed on your eyeball.

ARTHUR: When it's done, we're gonna feel better about what happened aren't we?

BANKS: A lot better.

ARTHUR: Let's find him now, get it over with.

BANKS: How do you make a soufflé?

ARTHUR: In the oven?

BANKS: Preparation. We have to learn to conquer our natures and not steam in like hot-heads. You make the mind run the body, not the other way round.

ARTHUR: But you're always flipping out. Someone looks at you wrong and you cut them.

BANKS: Think Jarrett in *White Heat* –

ARTHUR: James Cagney on top of the gas tank?

BANKS: (*Nodding.*) Think he got to be the boss of a gang by being reasonable?

Pause.

A little craziness keeps everybody in line.

ARTHUR: When have you made a soufflé?

ART SCHOOL PARTY – STUDENT HOUSE, EVENING

The Band in the corner of the living room plays soul funk with hits from '68 scratched in. Art school boys try and look cool. Girls do a formation 'Tales of the Unexpected' go-go dance around an enormous mountain of handbags. Band plays quietly under the dialogue.

CELIE and her boyfriend JETHRO, 19 and small, smooch onto the stage. She leads and JETHRO stands on her feet the way a child stands on an adult's when dancing.

CELIE: Staring out the back of the bus like a little nodding dog.

JETHRO: You did what was best for him.

CELIE: He hates me for it.

JETHRO: You want to be right and popular? Come on, let's get you a snakebite.

CELIE and JETHRO dance off the stage.

MOZ walks into the party, carrying a Watney Party Seven. He looks around. ROX, with a beehive and make-up applied with a trowel, heads straight for him.

ROX: Bastard!

MOZ: Bastard? You never wrote to me once while I were –

ROX: Sharon Sugar!

MOZ: What? –

ROX: Sharon Sugar, you were shagging Sharon Sugar.

MOZ: I never –

ROX: You were walking me home and then going round to Sharon Sugar's!

MOZ: Bollocks…as if… She lives with her Mam and Dad how could I –

ROX: She'd give you a piggy-back upstairs so they'd only hear one lot of footsteps!

MOZ: She always had a gob on her.

Pause.

It were only once –

ROX: A night.

MOZ: Rox… Roxy Foxy –

ROX: Not listening. Must have needed my head examining going out with you.

MOZ: It's me who needs my head examining.

Pause.

Look at you, gorgeous, how could I –

ROX: Shag Sharon Sugar? No wonder she could carry you, she's built like a wrestler.

MOZ: Is she here?

ROX: No. She's gone on her holidays to Denmark. Who goes to Denmark? She's probably coming back as a man. –

MOZ: Can't believe I nearly chucked away the chance of being with Roxy Farmer.

ROX: Not falling for it. –

MOZ: I knew you'd have hidden talents. You at art school now?

ROX: Still at the shoe factory

Pause.

I've been promoted, I'm on insoles now.

MOZ: It's fate then. What's the chance of me and you meeting at an art school party? You a finisher and me –

ROX: A lying, cheating, two-faced turd. You're only here cause there's no girls left round our way who don't know what you're like!

MOZ: I'm here because you're here.

Pause.

Give us another chance.

Reaches over and pulls a Saint Christopher out of the top of her jumper.

Still wearing it.

ROX: Paid for it.

MOZ: Chose it together.

ROX: And I had to pay for the clothes you ordered too. You're blacklisted from me Mum's catalogue.

MOZ: I'd have paid if… I didn't get sent down on purpose… I've missed you.

ROX: (*Thawing.*) Have you?

MOZ: Yeah. Really.

Pause.

There's a moon tonight…not as good as the one over Farnley res. –

ROX: Thought we were gonna get caught when that dog came up sniffing.

MOZ: Let's go for a walk. –

ROX: Didn't nick these shoes to walk in. What do you wanna…

Pause.

Oh I get it, a WALK.

MOZ: An old times' sake WALK.

ROX reaches up and unfastens the Saint Christopher.

ROX: Not even half a bitter. Couldn't even buy me half a bitter.

Pause.

Go for a walk on your own.

MOZ: Been going for a WALK on me own for five years!

ROX: Well swim over to Denmark and ask Sharon Sugar for a piggy-back then.

ROX drops the Saint Christopher into his palm.

Patron Saint of Travellers, he'll keep you company.

Pause.

Hope you don't drown.

MOZ: Think you're a lady 'cause you're at a posh party?

ROX: Think I deserve better than you.

ROX walks off swinging her hips.

MOZ looks around the room for more prey. Spots the prettiest girl, JENNIFER, 21. She swigs vodka. MOZ goes and joins her.

MOZ: Is heaven missing an angel then? Must be if you're here…

JENNIFER: (*Winces.*) Ouch!

MOZ: Worked last time I used it.

JENNIFER: When was that, the Blitz? (*Posh accent.*) 'A terrible war but we were damn plucky and we got through it!'

JENNIFER takes a hit of vodka.

MOZ: Women have changed.

JENNIFER: What do you mean?

MOZ: Been away for a while…and you lot have changed.

JENNIFER: When you left were we balancing books on our head and practising etiquette?

MOZ: You weren't swigging vodka…couldn't even go to the bog on your own.

JENNIFER: I'm not on my own, I've got mates here…they're in the kitchen debating the merits of Floyd without Syd Barrett.

MOZ: What?

JENNIFER: You a visitor from out of space then? Dr Who without his Tardis.

Band strikes up pop song.

(*Sings.*) Yesterday's man
You don't understand
No need to be a he man
You could be a free man
Yesterday's man
You don't understand
Now the girls wear the trousers
And the boys wear the blouses
Yesterday's man

MOZ: (*Singing.*) Baby, you're the one to save me
Heal me, maybe help me find the real me

JENNIFER: (*Singing.*) Yesterday's man
Mr Five-year Plan
What you need to do is let go
Of your id and your ego
In your Beatle suit
You look quite cute

There's just one thing though
You've got a nose like Ringo

MOZ: (*Singing.*) Baby, you're the one to save me
Heal me, maybe help me find the real me

Music continues quietly under dialogue.

No boyfriend then?

JENNIFER shakes her head.

No fiancée that's going to come out of the loo and belt me?

JENNIFER: Don't believe in marriage.

MOZ: Thoroughly modern.

JENNIFER: Still stuck with being a bridesmaid for my cousin
though. Least you get the dress without the drip of a
husband…and it's compulsory to get off, for one evening
only, with someone entirely unsuitable.

MOZ: Like me?

JENNIFER: We're not at a wedding.

MOZ: But I'd never do for a posh girl like you…

JENNIFER: Who said I was posh?

MOZ: Your accent.

JENNIFER: You don't choose what you're born into.

MOZ: What does your Dad do?

JENNIFER: Expects to be waited on hand and foot and treats
me like a ten year old. That's why I moved out as soon as I
got into college.

MOZ: Your own flat, you could help the homeless.

JENNIFER: How?

MOZ: Take me home with you.

JENNIFER: What's wrong with your own home?

MOZ: You know when you're little and you think your Mum is always gonna make you a Bovril...

Pause.

It's bollocks.

JENNIFER: (*Mocking.*) Ah...had a bust up then?

MOZ: Could say that.

JENNIFER: We never have rows in our house, my parents have perfected the art of the prolonged sulk. He has the lounge, she has the living room and never the twain shall meet.

Pause.

The only thing they ever bond on is how much they hate my friends.

MOZ: Is there just you?

JENNIFER: Got an older sister. Unhappily married to a bottle of vodka. My parents find that less embarrassing than me being part of the anti-war movement.

JENNIFER takes a shot of vodka.

To Mater and Pater!

JENNIFER passes the bottle to MOZ.

MOZ: And to Sisters!

JENNIFER: If my Father knew where I was going tonight he'd lose the last three hairs of his comb-over; I'm off to London for the anti-war demo.

MOZ: You don't want to go to London, it's full of Londoners and we were just getting to know each other.

JENNIFER: We're going to blockade the American Embassy.

MOZ: Why?

JENNIFER: 'Cause America shouldn't be in Vietnam.

Pause.

The Vietnamese resent being invaded and they know the ground better than the Americans. The US can't win so it acts like a toddler, throws an armed strop.

MOZ: You've said that before.

JENNIFER: Never to you.

Pause.

Come…come with us.

MOZ: You going to abduct me, strip me naked and brainwash me till I join your communist cell?

JENNIFER: In your dreams.

MOZ: I've nowhere else to go so…

JENNIFER: I'll go and bags you a place in the van, it'll be a bit of a squash.

MOZ: Hate war, love a squash.

JENNIFER goes.

CELIE and JETHRO come into the room carrying drinks. CELIE storms up to MOZ, JETHRO follows sheepishly.

CELIE: Look what the cat's dragged in!

MOZ: I promised to get on the coach, didn't say how long I'd stay on it.

CELIE: Don't give a shit about anybody else do you? You've always been the same, even as a kid, it was always whatever you wanted and screw everybody else.

MOZ: Like what?

CELIE: Like never helping at home, like not letting me walk home from school with you.

MOZ: As if I'd let me little brainbox of a sister tag along.

CELIE: Why do you think I wanted to walk home with you? What do you think it was like to come top of the class in a school full of psychos? I spent every break time hiding in the bogs or getting hammered and you never even noticed...my big popular brother, everybody's mate, except mine.

MOZ: Oh I noticed.

CELIE: If you noticed...why didn't you...

MOZ: Ah, did the little Princess get a touch of reality? You were always the favourite, they'd wave your reports in front of me nose. 'Look how hard your little Sister works'...nobody asked me if I wanted to go to university. There was stuff I was good at...

CELIE: Upsetting Dad, disappointing Mum...don't do degrees in that.

MOZ: Bitch.

CELIE: Least I'm not a killer.

MOZ: Screw you!

CELIE: Nobody wants you here.

MOZ: Good, I'm going to London.

JENNIFER comes in.

JENNIFER: (*Shouting from across the room.*) The van's outside! Anybody going to the London demo better get their arses into gear!

CELIE: (*Looking at JENNIFER.*) I should have known. Won't do anything his family asks but goes all the way to London to get his end away.

MOZ: Well it's further away from you...

CELIE: Wants a bit of rough does she? Well you've met your match there, she collects hearts does Miss Student Radical…you'll be alright, you don't have one.

JENNIFER: (*Directing it at MOZ.*) Last call for London Express, anybody going to the demo has to move it now.

CELIE: As if you give a shit about war.

MOZ: I've been locked up remember. How would you know what I give a shit about?

Pause.

Least I'm willing to admit that I'm going because I want to get laid, not like you using Banks as an excuse to get me out of the way. Scared I might want me bedroom back?

JETHRO: That's enough…you're behaving like kids.

MOZ: Button it!

CELIE: Shut it!

MOZ and JENNIFER and half the room leave the party.

CELIE gulps her drink down.

JETHRO: That went well.

CELIE: Drives me mad.

JETHRO: Could see the resemblance.

CELIE: Round the eyes?

JETHRO: Pair of hotheads.

CELIE: Did you hear what he called me?

JETHRO: (*Nodding.*) Heard what you called him.

CELIE: I know, it's always been the same… I want to tell him I've missed him and what comes out is sod off.

Pause.

Come on, let's get drunk.

JETHRO and CELIE head towards the kitchen and leave the stage.

ARTHUR walks into the party. Surveys the room, the music starts to get to him and he begins to tap his foot.

BANKS wheels himself in.

BANKS: Don't practise your footwork here.

ARTHUR: The music, just gets to you dun't it?

BANKS: Only if you're an imbecile. Give up tapping your foot. I'm sensitive to vibrations, it's giving me headache.

BANKS grabs a bottle of wine off a passing student. When the lad goes as if to protest, BANKS growls and the lad scuttles off.

(*Taking a swig.*) Top of the world, Mama.

Looking around.

Degenerates. That's pop culture for you. Ten years ago these arseholes would be sat at home in a cardigan and slippers. Look at 'em now, think they can reinvent the world 'cause they've got a record player.

BANKS gets a bottle of Dexedrine out and necks one.

ARTHUR: Probably pisses you off more 'cause you can't dance.

BANKS: I can dance, just choose to keep me syncopations to meself.

ARTHUR: No shame in admitting that you can't dance. I can't make me tongue touch the tip of me nose.

Tries and fails.

Can't be good at everything.

BANKS wheels his chair out on to the dance floor. BANKS holds himself still for a moment waiting to catch the beat and then does a fantastic and complicated hand jive perfectly in time to the music.

People in the room begin to clap along. CELIE and JETHRO enter the room to see what all the fuss is about, BANKS spots them abandons his performance mid-clap.

BANKS wheels himself over to them.

People stare at him confused.

BANKS: Move along, nothing to see here! Yeah, I'm in a chair! What's your problem?

ARTHUR joins BANKS.

(*To CELIE.*) Oi Gretel, where's Hansel hiding?

BANKS slips a knife out.

We're going outside to look at the constellations.

CELIE: I don't want to.

BANKS shows her the knife.

BANKS: Yeah you do, bit of frost reveals the heavens. Get your arse moving, or you or your Diddy man here, whichever one I can get to first, will be limping into the morgue. One cut to the right artery and you'll be squirting all over the Axminster.

To ARTHUR.

See there's a reason you should always take the carpet up at parties.

BANKS, ARTHUR, CELIE and JETHRO all move outside. The stage is dark.

CELIE: It's pointless asking us, we don't know where he is.

BANKS: (*Pointing up.*) Ursa Major, big dipper, the great bear. Those seven stars mean someat different to every civilisation.

Pause.

The Arabs, the Greeks, the Aztecs…foreigners, fuck 'em!
Story I like's anonymous, see that…that's a pan on a fire,
and that little dot on the handle is a bloke sitting there
waiting for it to boil. Know what happens when it does?

ARTHUR: He makes a brew?

BANKS: No he doesn't make a brew!

Pause.

When that pan boils it's the end of the world.

ARTHUR: Why?

BANKS: Just is.

ARTHUR: Why?

BANKS: 'Cause I say it is. Keep up Arthur.

Pause.

Are you two engaged?

CELIE: No.

BANKS: No engagement ring?

*CELIE shakes her head and flashes her left hand to show there is no
ring. BANKS grabs her hand.*

(*To CELIE, looking at her hand.*) Not done much washing up.

(*To ARTHUR.*) Hold her hand out straight.

ARTHUR takes CELIE's hand and holds it out.

CELIE: What you doing?

BANKS: Giving you a manicure.

To JETHRO.

I so much as see you blink without asking permission and
I'll take it out on your girlfriend's hand.

*BANKS opens his bag of tricks and takes out a pair of garden secateurs.
CELIE cries out.*

If trees cried would we still sever branches?

Pause.

Yeah. Never could stand whingers.

CELIE: What you doing?

BANKS: I'm just gonna ask you where Moz is once and if you
don't say I'm going to cut a finger off. And if you don't
actually know, tough shit, some days just don't work out.

CELIE struggles.

Where is he?

JETHRO: (*Blurting it out.*) He's gone down to London in a van,
there's a big anti-war demo, Grosvenor Square. He'll be
easy to spot, he'll be the only one wearing a suit.

ARTHUR drops CELIE's hand.

CELIE: (*To JETHRO.*) You could have just said where he'd gone.

BANKS: (*To JETHRO.*) Empty your pockets.

*JETHRO empties his pockets. There is a pound note, car keys and a
packet of condoms.*

(*Waving the condoms.*) Prophylactics…

CELIE gives JETHRO a dirty look.

JETHRO: (*To CELIE.*) It's our Brian's coat…they were just in the
pocket.

BANKS: (*To JETHRO.*) You've got car keys so don't bother giving
me any bollocks about not having a motor. Go get it and
your girlfriend can stay here and keep us company.

JETHRO points to a battered old car that stands beside them.

That heap of scrap metal! Thank God it's dark.

JETHRO: The clutch sticks so you've got to be –

BANKS: Only thing I've got to be mate is well dressed; YOU'RE driving us to London.

JETHRO: But I've been drinking!

BANKS: Can walk, can drive.

BANKS pops another pill. BANKS gets in and a reluctant JETHRO gets into the driving seat.

ARTHUR loads BANKS' wheelchair. They have a conversation as he does it.

(*To ARTHUR.*) What's the face for?

ARTHUR: There's no face.

BANKS: You've either shat yourself or you've got someat you want to spit out.

ARTHUR: I didn't know you were gonna do his sister.

JETHRO: That were out of order.

BANKS: If I wanted Jiminy Cricket's opinion I'd give a little whistle; until then, keep it shut.

ARTHUR: All that business with the fingers.

BANKS: Fear's good currency.

ARTHUR gets in the car.

ARTHUR: But a girl.

BANKS: There's a revolution in motion, read the papers, they're forming fucking feminist collectives.

ARTHUR: They're not demanding to have their fingers cut off.

BANKS: Equality means taking the rough with the smooth.

The car engine chokes and dies.

JETHRO: What's wrong with it?

BANKS: This is an Italian suit not an overall.

JETHRO: It doesn't like hills.

BANKS: It hasn't got a personality, it's a machine, inanimate and ugly. Get out and fix it!

Scared, JETHRO gets out and tinkers with the engine. He pulls various springs and screws out and hits the engine with things intermittently.

BANKS and ARTHUR just sit in the car waiting.

(*Shouting.*) You haven't a clue have you?

JETHRO: No.

BANKS: Why the gala performance?

JETHRO: I'm an art student…my fingers.

ARTHUR: Let's go home, we'll follow them tomorrow.

BANKS: Napoleon never just went home.

ARTHUR: He probably didn't live as close as us.

BANKS: Get the chair…

As ARTHUR unloads, BANKS breaks into song, backed by band, with ARTHUR and JETHRO humming doo-wop underneath.

ARTHUR: (*Singing.*) What are we gonna do now?

BANKS: (*Singing.*) Brothers gonna work it out, brothers gonna work it out…

ARTHUR: We're gonna hitchhike!

BANKS: (*Singing.*) Stand up tall, stick out that thumb
Don't put it down till kingdom comes
We don't need no railway station
To take us to our destination
… We're gonna hitch hike!

Got an itch no quack can diagnose

No rest till the boy is comatose
Blood red moon for company
This grudge will surely carry me
… We're gonna hitch hike!

Gonna go to where the road meets sky
And when we get there, that boy gonna die
This pick me up's got no turning back
We're gonna hit that road like Kerouac

… We're gonna hitch hike!

BACK OF A TRANSIT NIGHT

The van is jam packed with bodies. Whisky and joints are being passed around. Someone farts and everyone covers their noses and looks round accusingly.

CARL: Ugh! Dog food! There's too many people in here. It's doing my head in. We should have had a vote on who got in the van.

JENNIFER: Carl's keen on voting.

CARL: If we'd had a show of hands we wouldn't have ended up with a spy in the van.

Points at MOZ.

Look at his haircut.

MOZ: Cheeky sod!

JENNIFER: He's not a spy.

CARL: Snooping round you at the party. We talked about this at the planning meeting…knew there would be police infiltrators, just didn't think we'd be bringing our own. I say that we dump him at the side of the road. –

MOZ: I'll dump you! –

JENNIFER: He's not a cop, he used to go out with my sister...
I've known him for years.

Pause.

None of you would be in this van if I hadn't booked it. (*To*
CARL.) You're always going on about attracting the working
class, just talk was it?

The van settles down. Everybody but MOZ and JENNIFER goes to
sleep.

MOZ: Thanks, you didn't need to do that.

JENNIFER: Maybe I shouldn't have. It is weird you just turning
up...you act like you've been in a coma.

MOZ: I've been away for a few years.

JENNIFER: Where?

MOZ: Would you believe travelling?

JENNIFER: Not with that haircut.

MOZ: See these shoes?

JENNIFER: New.

MOZ: Bought 'em today, first pair for years that haven't been
worn in by somebody else first. Other men's shoes shape
the way you walk...never yourself in dead men's shoes.

JENNIFER: Don't buy second-hand shoes then.

MOZ: Prison issue. Just got out today.

JENNIFER: How long did you do?

MOZ: Five years.

JENNIFER: You don't get five years for stealing a jar of coffee!

MOZ holds his head and does not say anything; finally, finally...

MOZ: I was the driver of a car that –

JENNIFER: You were a getaway driver! –

MOZ: I was driving –

JENNIFER: A bank job! That's SO cool. You didn't shoot anybody did you?

MOZ: I didn't shoot anybody.

JENNIFER cuddles up to him.

JENNIFER: A bank robber. I'm going on a demo with a BLACK bank robber!

MOZ: Why are we going on a demo? We could have stayed at the party and got pissed.

JENNIFER: We can get drunk here.

MOZ: Bollocks this innit?

JENNIFER: No.

MOZ: You're all just playing at it.

JENNIFER: Even if we were, so what? Vietnam matters but nobody's pretending it's just that.

MOZ: What is it then? Trying to piss your parents off?

JENNIFER: Don't need to get in a van to do that.

Pause.

You know there are days that are meant to be special, like your 21st or New Year's Eve, and they're actually a bit crap. Well this year, nearly every day's felt like something…like something brilliant's happening –

MOZ: That's drugs and music for you.

JENNIFER: They help but it's not just that…it's like we're all switched on, like we can do anything we want: take over the schools, fuck in the road. Whatever! Time's speeding up, whatever history is supposed to be, well I think this is it.

MOZ: You wanna do it in the road?

JENNIFER: Nah, too cold on my ass.

Pause.

At the party, I saw you arguing with Celie Morris.

MOZ: Little Sister.

JENNIFER: I've seen her stuff, she's a good painter.

MOZ: She should be.

JENNIFER: Meaning?

MOZ: Swot.

JENNIFER: It got her into college.

MOZ: They were always going to send her to college.

Pause.

Mum and Dad always made a big fuss of Celie.

JENNIFER: Bet they made a big fuss of you too, only you were too busy trying to look at girls' knickers to remember.

MOZ: I missed seeing my quota of pants for quite a few years, thank you very much, too busy carting my little sister around.

JENNIFER: Bet they had a field day with you in the prison showers.

MOZ: Sympathetic aren't you?

JENNIFER: Don't get all soppy on me, I'm not that sort of girl. I'm messed up, got my own problems, I don't do sympathy.

JENNIFER and MOZ lapse into silence. The Band strikes up a blues tune.

Someone passes them a joint. MOZ takes a toke and coughs.

Don't cough, you don't get off.

MOZ puts his arms around her.

MOZ: (*Inhaling.*) Most comforting thing in the world being wrapped around a woman.

JENNIFER: Any woman?

MOZ: One whose hair smells like cherries.

JENNIFER turns to him. They kiss lightly.

Sorry…

JENNIFER: We all whinge sometimes, it's alright.

MOZ: Didn't mean that, I feel sick…it's the dope… I'm not used to it…has anybody got a carrier bag?

SIDE OF THE MOTORWAY NIGHT

BANK's wheelchair is hidden behind a big bush. We hear only his voice. ARTHUR stands at the side of the motorway hitching. The sound and shadows of cars going past fill the night.

A fox shrieks.

BANKS: You've got to have respect for a creature can make a noise like that; half the battle is front.

ARTHUR: What do you think it were?

BANKS: Wolf. Look over there, see them two pin-pricks of light? It's out there watching us, waiting.

ARTHUR: What for?

BANKS: For us to nod off, drop off for a second and it'll be over here ripping us apart, chewing on our entrails.

ARTHUR: But there's a bacon factory over there, it could just go through the bins for the scraps.

BANKS: Warm fresh meat, nothing beats it apparently. Resourceful creatures wolves, show more ferocity than is needed, keeps men scared.

ARTHUR: Let's go home.

BANKS: It's a fox, knobhead.

ARTHUR: But you said it was a –

BANKS: Psychology. How do you think magic works? What we do is an illusion, we're mere men who must appear as fucking gods.

ARTHUR: Don't wanna be a god, I just wanna go home.

BANKS: I'm speaking metaphorically.

ARTHUR: We've been here ages…if we don't get picked up in the next ten cars I'm setting off back.

BANKS: Tintin wouldn't just go home.

ARTHUR: Thought you didn't like me reading comics? –

Pause.

And Tintin didn't have a prick of a brother reckoning to be a wolf or Jesus or whatever…and he had Snowy and Captain Haddock backing him up.

BANKS: I'm worth ten Belgium cartoon fuckers.

ARTHUR: No-one's gonna stop.

Pause.

Cars going past…keep thinking about our Kath. –

BANKS: Wasn't a car that killed out Kath. It was Moz.

ARTHUR: If I hadn't been having me appendix out that night –

BANKS: If Jupiter hadn't been aligned with Mars, if the moon were made of cheese, if I had two good legs…where do IFs get us?

ARTHUR: Nowhere.

BANKS: You being in hospital had nothing to do with it. Only circumstance could have stopped our Kath dying was if that pillock Moz hadn't been showing off –

ARTHUR: You tried to stop him –

BANKS: 'Course I did. Only time I've ever begged. Got in that car to talk some sense into him.

ARTHUR: He were too pissed to listen. You did everything you could.

Pause.

At the funeral…you never cried.

BANKS: Tears are no measure of feeling.

ARTHUR: When you were a kid, when you had the accident, did you cry then?

BANKS: Is there a point to this?

ARTHUR: It's just I've never seen you…all them operations on your legs, and Mam and Dad and our Kath…it might make you…less…if you –

BANKS: Less what?

ARTHUR: Less y'know.

BANKS: No idea what you're talking about.

A Ford Anglia car pulls up. A middle-aged couple sit up front.

DRIVER: Nearly missed you in the dark.

ARTHUR rushes to get BANKS.

ARTHUR: (*Shouting.*) Just me…and my brother.

WOMAN: We weren't going to stop…but our son's a student… he's been all round the world –

DRIVER: On his thumb. –

WOMAN: Thought we should…it's awfully late… I said to Maurice, could be Brian by the –

ARTHUR pulls wheelchair out.

ARTHUR: Thanks, we're freezing, been here hours.

DRIVER: But –

WOMAN: I don't think it's a good idea to –

BANKS: What, is it too much trouble to give a guy in a wheelchair a lift? –

BANKS gets himself in the car, while ARTHUR puts the wheelchair on the roof. ARTHUR gets in during next speech.

DRIVER: It's just that –

BANKS: You should think yourself lucky that anybody is willing to travel in this mortification of a car. Why would any man in his right mind buy a Ford Anglia? It screams low self-esteem, it begs to be cut up, forced off the road… it says, whatever you do to me I won't make a fuss because I'm a little guy with no aspirations. In short, Sir…you're a loser.

DRIVER: But –

WOMAN: I chose the car –

BANKS: And you admit it?

DRIVER: But –

BANKS: But what?

DRIVER: We're only going to the next junction.

ARTHUR messes with the radio dial – the Band going through musical genres – and the DRIVER and his WIFE get out. As ARTHUR settles on an appropriate station a new driver, MARY, an attractive, bit prim twenty-something gets in.

BANKS is in the back, chewing, speeding and pissed off.

MARY: Sandwich?

ARTHUR: Great, I'm starving.

MARY: (*Points backwards at BANKS.*) By his feet.

BANKS: What feet? –

ARTHUR: (*Hissing.*) Give up!

ARTHUR picks up a tupperware box.

MARY: Fish paste. (*To BANKS.*) With beetroot. Do you want one too?

BANKS: Fish paste and beetroot, and they say the British cuisine is limited.

ARTHUR: My brother doesn't eat.

MARY: What, ever?

BANKS: I'm still here, much as you might wish it, I haven't grown wings and flown out the back window.

BANKS pops a hand full of speed pills with a hip flask.

Made it Ma, Top of the world!

ARTHUR: Don't take any more dexys.

BANKS: Why?

ARTHUR: You've had enough.

BANKS: That's an opinion.

ARTHUR: This lady might not like you taking drugs in her car.

MARY: Is it medicine?

BANKS: Yeah.

MARY: My cousin's in a wheelchair.

BANKS: We must be related.

MARY: I didn't mean… I was just making…have you always been, y'know, in a wheel chair? –

ARTHUR: My brother doesn't like talking about it.

BANKS: No, it's alright, it's fine, most people just wonder without asking. Never ask, never find out. Little kid when it happened, five years old…our Mam took us to Blackpool zoo…baby Arthur there was in his pram…but me I was on the reins, little red coat with a velvet collar and balaclava that my Grandma knit. All morning I'm like a little cherub holding onto that pram, I'm OOOing and AHHHing at lions and tigers and bears and hiding behind our Mam's legs if anything so much as sneezed, so our Mam takes the reins off while we have our butties. She's fiddling with the bottle for Arthur and I see a giant kingfisher standing on a mound…proudest brightest bird I have ever seen. You cannot beat the kingfisher for fucking majesty.

Pause.

I go straight for the gate into the compound, one push and it opens…the kingfisher's above a pool, admiring its reflection, and who could blame it, eh? I waddle over and just as I get to it…out of the water slides this giant crocodile and SNAP. SNAP! Both my fucking legs.

MARY: Oh God, that's awful.

BANKS: Yeah and I'm lying in this bloody puddle and the tooth fairy dive bombs and starts whacking me with her wand.

ARTHUR: My brother was hit by a bus, when he was eight, he was hit by a bus.

BANKS: And my vocal chords were miraculously undamaged so I'll speak for meself if you don't mind!

MARY: I shouldn't have asked.

BANKS: Woman who picks two strange men up on a dark stretch of road –

ARTHUR: Give up.

BANKS: Woman who does that is either reckless or asking for something. –

ARTHUR: Stop it! –

BANKS: Be rude not to find out why she wants two men in her car in the middle of the night. She's wondering if my soldier can stand up to attention when he hears the call to arms. Might look like she's starched her bloomers but –

MARY: I'm a Christian. I stopped because I'm a Christian.

BANKS: Well wash my feet!

ARTHUR: There's no need for it!

BANKS: True.

MARY gets out. ARTHUR tunes the radio dial as he speaks. BANKS pops another pill.

ARTHUR: You didn't have to do that. She were doing us a favour and you went out your way to freak her out, she were nice and –

BANKS: Nice! Women are mercenaries, pick you off as look at you. –

ARTHUR: Always have to go too far. Even as a kid, anybody looked at you sideways and you'd have 'em…they didn't even have to look, they just had to have something you wanted.

Pause.

Always had to be Top Dog.

BANKS: Too right, what do you think a kid with no legs ends up being if he's not Top Dog?

ARTHUR: And if he's always Top Dog what does he end up being then?

BANKS: I don't know what you're on the rag about, she was just a woman.

ARTHUR: She was nice and you scared her.

BANKS: Couldn't take a joke, you don't want to end up being saddled with a woman who can't take a joke.

ARTHUR: I were talking to her.

BANKS: Talk to me.

Pause.

Don't mean to be grumpy, my legs hurt.

ARTHUR: I know.

Gently.

Let me stick to the bottle of dexys for you.

BANKS: (*Passes bottle to ARTHUR.*) If I ask for 'em though, I get 'em back straight away.

ARTHUR: Get your breath. I'll give 'em you back if you want 'em.

BANKS: Shouldn't have coffee after six, that's what does it. I'll balance the dexys out with a Mandrax.

Takes a Mandrax.

I'm a pussy cat after a Mandrax.

BANKS is drowsy through next speech which goes on as ARTHUR tunes the radio dial.

Moodiness in a woman, the monthlies; moodiness in a man, sign of genius. Julius Caesar…why the long face? Napoleon, not a door on its hinges, Lucky Luciano, you didn't wake him up before twelve…and Ronnie Kray, look at him wrong and…

BANKS falls asleep.

The Band plays an umpaah tune. The next driver, besuited businessman, RICHARD gets in. He brings a great bag of balloons with him, which he lets loose in the car.

RICHARD: Sorry about the balloons, I'm in them. Functions, we supply functions, with balloons. Got to be in Watford first thing, conference, last minute job, they want 200 balloons first thing... I've only had chance to do about ten. I'm on my last warning at work, if I don't have 200 by morning...you couldn't do me a massive favour and blow us up a few could you?

ARTHUR: What now, in the car?

RICHARD nods.

ARTHUR picks a balloon up, begins to blow, knots the end. RICHARD watches, licks his lips. ARTHUR does another.

RICHARD: Bigger...you couldn't do it bigger could you? They want big balloons.

RICHARD squirms in his seat, excited as ARTHUR blows. The balloon gets bigger and bigger.

There's a pump, by your feet, it's already got a balloon attached...use the pump.

ARTHUR starts to use the pump.

Make it as big as it will go. God, that's so big, it's huge... I don't know how I'm going to get that...keep pumping, don't stop! That's so good, it's so so big, keep pumping, keep, don't stop! –

The balloon bursts as RICHARD ejaculates. BANKS wakes up with a start.

BANKS: What! Jesus! What the...

BANKS bursts all the balloons in a temper as ARTHUR tunes the radio dial. RICHARD gets out.

ARTHUR: Just a balloon... I was helping him...for a conference.

BANKS: Conference! Give us me dexys, I need to be on guard duty.

ARTHUR: Go back to sleep.

BANKS: What so I can wake up to find you dressed as a Bavarian milk maid while some jerk tosses off into a cream horn? Why did you let him get so freaky with you? Conference!

ARTHUR: No harm done.

BANKS: (*Popping pill.*) No harm! Harm's not a bad thing, lack of respect, that's what's to be feared. That tit had no respect for you!

Pause.

Reggie Kray wouldn't have fallen for that.

ARTHUR: Think the Krays have any real mates?

BANKS: Loads. Only crew that counts in the East End.

ARTHUR: I mean someone who isn't shitting themselves.

BANKS: Each other, they've got each other, like we have, like James Cagney had...

ARTHUR: That's a film...and he killed himself.

BANKS: Brilliant ending that. Cagney never had a better role.

ARTHUR: Can you remember Colin Fry?

BANKS: Did he leap off a gas tank?

ARTHUR: No. He was my best mate.

BANKS: I'm your best mate, I'm your brother.

ARTHUR: Used to wait outside my classroom for me.

BANKS: Did he have a bike?

ARTHUR: Yeah, a Raleigh.

BANKS: Quality bike that. Craftsmanship.

ARTHUR: You said he had to give it to you.

BANKS: What would I want a bike for? –

ARTHUR: And he wouldn't 'cause that bike were all his birthdays and Christmases put together.

BANKS: Expensive, Raleighs.

ARTHUR: You told me you needed the wheels for a cart, made me take it off him, I had to bust his face to get it.

BANKS: Can't remember having a cart.

ARTHUR: 'Cause you never made one…you shoved the bike in the canal. You made me choose between you and Colin Fry and you didn't even want it.

BANKS: Kids eh?

The Band strikes up a mournful blues grass tune.

ARTHUR: (*Singing.*) Dear brother, dear brother
How long will this take
'Cause I'm so tired of dealing
With your growing pains
Gonna go ride the railroad
Gonna leave you some day
Please forgive me for not going
Your way

BANKS: (*Singing.*) I remember all the fights
And you stood up for me
'Cause so many times they wanted
To step right on me
'Cause me and my brother
My brother and me

And I know that's how it's gonna
Always be

Then the two verses sung together as a round robin. As they reach the end of the tune the lighting changes to lava lamp frenzy, the music becomes psychedelic, the balloons are pushed out of the car and TREEFROG gets in. Mid-thirties, she could be attractive if she wasn't wearing garish clown pants and a strange contraption on her head. Her headgear is made out of coat hangers with crystals attached.

BANKS: Talking of fucking Bavarian milk maids.

TREEFROG passes ARTHUR a fly swot.

TREEFROG: I'm going to London.

ARTHUR: We're going to London… I'm Arthur and that's my brother, Banks.

TREEFROG: I'm Treefrog. Treefrog Pendragon.

BANKS: Jesus, we're on our way to Middle Earth.

Pause.

You must hate your parents. (*Referring to name.*) Sadists.

TREEFROG: Eileen…they called me Eileen. Don't think it suits me anymore. Everything from my old life's going. Just trying Treefrog out, haven't settled on it yet, seeing if it fits.

ARTHUR: Why Treefrog?

TREEFROG: Have you seen their eyes? Life's startled them. I want to be amazed by life… I'm experimenting.

Pause.

Can you erm see…anything…sort of buzzing around and settling on the dash?

ARTHUR: Like a fly? –

BANKS: No flies about at night, twelve hours sleep they need every day. Exhausting being a parasite.

TREEFROG: I don't mean flies exactly…sort of something different.

ARTHUR: Like what?

TREEFROG: (*Unsure.*) Like little shrunken cops with wings?

ARTHUR shakes his head.

I thought I was imagining them…but better to check.

ARTHUR: If you don't mind me asking, are you high?

TREEFROG: Well, I'm not low.

ARTHUR: Let's stop and get a cup of coffee.

TREEFROG: Coffee's bad for you –

BANKS: My thoughts exactly –

TREEFROG: I've had some tea anyway…mushrooms tea… a friend gave it to me, never had that sort before; much prefer it to Typhoo.

Points to a bag.

There's a flask in there if you'd –

ARTHUR: No, I'm alright.

TREEFROG: Could you pour me another cup?

BANKS: No!

TREEFROG: Very authoritative.

Turns around.

Has anybody ever told you you've got very dark eyes?

BANKS: All the better to see you with.

TREEFROG: And you're funny.

BANKS: I'm not the plonker with a coat hanger on me head.

TREEFROG: It was a coat hanger and now it's a vibe-a-thon…
these are healing crystals. They absorb dark thoughts and
emanate light.

TREEFROG taps headgear lightly so the crystals tinkle.

It's on the blink.

BANKS: No! I was just about to give to charity!

TREEFROG: My mother always warned me away from men
like you.

BANKS: Good. –

TREEFROG: Made you seem all the more exotic.

BANKS: I'll stick a pineapple on the wheelchair.

TREEFROG: What wheelchair?

Pause.

I'm not normally this…have you ever had mushrooms?
When I got in the car it seemed very important to stop the
war…now I'm just enjoying driving… I like the way the
white lines go all curvy and shoot off up to the stars.

Pause.

My husband wouldn't let me learn to drive. He wasn't a
nice man, he seemed like a nice man, my mother thought
he was a catch…she should have married him.

Pause.

We were very respectable. And very miserable. So when
we got divorced I thought…

ARTHUR: Live a little?

TREEFROG: Precisely.

Pause.

Your eyes aren't as deep as his. Are you sure you don't want some tea?

ARTHUR: Can't. We're looking for somebody.

TREEFROG: Why?

ARTHUR: He did a bad thing…

TREEFROG: Then when you find him, forgive him. –

BANKS: We'll tear him a new arsehole, that's what we'll do.

TREEFROG: I've forgiven my husband…he kept the milk and the toilet paper in his study…if I wanted milk in my tea or paper… I had to ask him…said he didn't like waste. –

ARTHUR: But he wasted his life. –

TREEFROG: Precisely. That's my new word.

BANKS: Could we have the drive without the commentary?

ARTHUR: Ignore him.

TREEFROG: I think he's funny.

Pause.

I'm taking my driving test next week.

BANKS: Don't bother practising the three-point-turn, just wear the coat hanger.

TREEFROG: Don't be scared of me.

BANKS: Me, scared? Never been afraid of anything.

TREEFROG: Everybody's afraid of something. Let go…

Pause.

I used to bleach my skirting boards.

Band strikes up psychedelic song.

(*Singing.*) Me and Icarus keep burning

So many things I'd like to try
Me and gravity are learning
What goes up now must stay high

Chorus
I just wanna fly
But I can't stop falling
But I can't stop falling
Always falling
I'm always falling

Verse
Tired of being my own darling
Another day of getting by
And I am not afraid of tumbling
'Cause I've already crossed that line

Chorus
I just wanna fly
But I can't stop falling
But I can't stop falling
Always falling
I'm always falling

OUTSIDE GROSVENOR SQUARE, LONDON MORNING

The stage is filled with noise, smoke and Klaxons. A police siren waxes and wanes.

JENNIFER and MOZ come on stage in a crowd of demonstrators. MOZ is swigging from a bottle of whisky.

JENNIFER holds her purse.

JENNIFER: (*Handing purse to MOZ.*) Will you put this in your pocket? I've nowhere to put it.

MOZ slips it into his trouser pocket, it bulges.

(*Eyeing bulge.*) A man of means.

A WOMAN dressed as cake wanders across the stage. She hands out free cake as she goes.

CAKE LADY: (*Shouting.*) Who gets the biggest slice of the cake? Red Ladder Theatre, Speakers' Corner, 3 o'clock.

CAKE LADY tries to hand a piece to MOZ.

MOZ: What's wrong with it?

CAKE LADY: Nothing.

MOZ: Why you giving it away then?

CAKE LADY: Imagine a world without money.

MOZ: Been living in it for years, it's shit.

CAKE LADY: Not one where you're more skint than everybody else; one where money doesn't exist.

CAKE LADY leaves the stage.

MOZ: Mental.

JENNIFER: Or sane, depends which way you look at it. You should have taken the cake…imagine everybody and everything free.

MOZ: My Dad was a socialist.

JENNIFER: He'd be proud of you then, coming here.

MOZ: Doubt it. He wasn't fighting for the right to be a victoria sponge.

JENNIFER: What happened to him?

MOZ: Dropped dead digging the roads. He'd turn in his grave if he saw this.

JENNIFER: Maybe he wouldn't, people like your Dad, they opened up this space for us. If they hadn't gone before, we wouldn't have the freedom –

MOZ: To be freaks –

JENNIFER: There's nothing wrong with being a freak, better than being –

MOZ: A screw or a cop.

JENNIFER: Suppose so...some of the cops will be alright though, you can't just tar them all with the same brush.

MOZ: You're funny, you want world-wide revolution and you defend cops.

JENNIFER: Just saying that they're not all bad.

MOZ: (*Looking round.*) Never seen so many cops.

JENNIFER: Thousands of them.

MOZ: What are they so worried about?

JENNIFER: That we'll burn the American Embassy to the ground.

MOZ: And will you?

JENNIFER: If we get the chance...and wouldn't that be embarrassing for international relations?

MOZ: Thought you didn't like violence?

JENNIFER: Five years inside and still don't know the difference between a few bricks and a human being?

MOZ: Failed me eleven plus; don't even know where Vietnam is.

JENNIFER: Next to China.

MOZ: Thought it was stuck on the side of America, like us and Wales. If it's miles away why should the yanks give a toss if a few Vietnamese became commies?

JENNIFER: Dominos, they think it's like dominos. One country falls to communism, then the next, then the...

MOZ: If it worked like that we'd all be calling each other Boyo.

The Band arrive on stage playing a New Orleans funeral tune. A HIPPY in vicar's vestments comes on followed by six undertakers in traditional garb carrying a coffin. Others follow rattling buckets for coins.

VICAR: (*Shouting.*) And young men, young black men are pushed to the front with targets pinned straight into their skins...deprived of health care and education so that their only future is no future and they –

TREEFROG pushes the coffin lid off and sits bolt upright in the coffin dressed as a skeleton.

TREEFROG: Oh yea! Oh yea! And on the third day she shall rise again!

VICAR: Not yet, not yet! Were not rising yet! You've ruined the theatrical experience! You're the horrific consequence of war...that needs a build up...you can't just appear. Get back in!

TREEFROG: I'm travel sick!

VICAR: Put her down. Put the coffin down. (*To TREEFROG.*) You've ruined it now.

The BEARERS put the coffin down.

TREEFROG: It's awfully stuffy in there.

VICAR: It's only five more minutes. How do you think the Vietcong feel, trapped in tunnels?

TREEFROG: And I need a wee!

VICAR: You won't get another chance to perform with us. You know Jack Nicholson was spotted doing street theatre!

TREEFROG climbs out.

Does anybody else want to rise again?

Looks at TREEFROG.

Somebody with a strong bladder who isn't claustrophobic. The world's full of out of work actors until you need one.

Shouts.

Anybody want to rise again? Ex-Italia Conti alumni need not apply.

Pause.

Oh sod it, we'll take anybody!

A band of HARI KRISHNAS dance on to the stage singing with bells and tambourines. They are followed by ARTHUR who dances behind them, hitting a cow bell.

MOZ spots ARTHUR on the other side of the street, MOZ looks for somewhere to run but sees nowhere.

HARI KRISHNAS: Hare Krishna Hare Krishna
Krishna Krishna Hare Hare
Hare Rama Hare Rama
Rama Rama Hare Hare

MOZ: I'll rise again! I'll do it!

MOZ jumps into the coffin.

TREEFROG: (*Running off stage clutching herself.*) Leave the lid off for him.

MOZ: I want the lid, put the lid on. (*To JENNIFER.*) Speakers' Corner, I'll meet you at Speakers' –

A COFFIN BEARER places the lid on. The Band stays stationary, playing a quiet tune under the dialogue.

BANKS pushes his wheelchair onto the stage. In the background the performers enact some sort of physical theatre with the coffin.

ARTHUR: (*Running over to BANKS.*) Bet the Queen's Coronation were like this, thousands of people –

BANKS: Where is he? Have you seen him?

ARTHUR: Who?

BANKS: Hairy Harry Christmas.

ARTHUR: I got sidetracked.

BANKS: I noticed.

> *Grabbing cow bell.*

> If there's one thing worse than a religious Nutter, it's a religious Nutter with a musical instrument.

> *Pause.*

> What do you think all these soap dodgers are doing here?

ARTHUR: Demonstrating. –

BANKS: As if this lot cared about a few Gooks!

ARTHUR: We're not meant to call them Gooks.

BANKS: Who says?

ARTHUR: (*Points to HIPPY GIRL.*) She said. Pisses 'em off; it's like someone calling you a cripple.

BANKS: They can call me what they like.

ARTHUR: You cut the last guy who called you a cripple.

BANKS: Never said I'd let 'em get away with it.

> *A line of COPS appear in black riot gear at each side of the stage, trapping the demonstrators in the centre.*

> *JENNIFER sits down in the road, other demonstrators follow suit and link arms, BANKS takes a run at them in his wheelchair and the CAKE LADY appears, grabs his chair and goes running off the side of the stage.*

CAKE LADY: (*Shouting.*) The cops are gonna charge!

BANKS: (*Screaming as he leaves.*) I'm being fucking kidnapped by a cake!

Cannisters of tear gas are thrown by the cops. The stage is covered with smoke. There is absolute confusion.

ARTHUR: Banks? Banks! Where's my brother? Banks!

JENNIFER grabs ARTHUR's sleeve and tugs him down.

JENNIFER: Get down, cover your face!

ARTHUR does as he is told.

A line of COPS appear on hobby horses and attack the crowd. Rearing over those sat down.

A hobby horse COP brings a baton down on JENNIFER's head, she manages to get her arms up there just in time, the COP brings the baton down again and ARTHUR grabs it and strikes the COP in the kneecaps so he falls.

Am I bleeding?

ARTHUR takes JENNIFER's face in his hands to examine her head, he shakes his head but instead of letting go he holds her face to his just a second too long, transfixed.

You hit a cop, we've gotta –

Another line of HOBBY HORSE COPS come forward, there is smoke everywhere. The Band strike up a tango tune. JENNIFER stands and grabs ARTHUR to lead him to safety, caught in the moment, ARTHUR grabs her and pulls her into his arms in one fluid Latin movement. He snaps his head from side to side, weighing up the opposition. Looks right into her eyes.

ARTHUR: We're surrounded.

JENNIFER: Cut off. No escape.

ARTHUR: Blistering barnacles.

JENNIFER: You read Tintin? I love Tintin.

ARTHUR: Head back, best foot forward, we're cutting a rug right through.

ARTHUR leads JENNIFER in a sensual tango through the police ranks. He throws her around and she loves it. It's magical and they cut a charmed way through. Rather than escaping off the stage, they get lost in each other and keep dancing. He dips her right back, pulls her to him and is just about to kiss her when a baton hits him on the back of the head. The tango ceases abruptly.

ARTHUR falls.

JENNIFER: Oh shit!

JENNIFER attempts to drag him unconscious back into the crowd, more COPS charge and she has to abandon him.

The CROWD start to stamp their feet beating out a rhythm as they chant.

CROWD: (*Repeatedly.*) Bin Bin Madam Bin!
Ho ho ho Chi Ming!

Under the stamping and chanting the Band strikes up a full on soul tune and the cops become troupe of soul dancers. They dance forward, pushing the crowd back and using their batons as props.

In a mock striptease the cops rip the numbers off their uniforms and throw them into the crowd.

One of the cops lays down a red carpet and out of the smoke dances TOP COP. He body pops along the carpet. His riot gear is silver and he has a giant quiff and burners.

A DEMONSTRATOR moon-walks in return. They have a little dance off.

BANKS wheels himself back on stage, round and round, frantically looking for ARTHUR whom he doesn't spot in the confusion.

TREEFROG enters.

TOP COP: (*Singing.*) Can I get a witness?

COP CHORUS: (*In response.*) Right on!

TOP COP: (*Singing.*) Can I get a witness?

COP CHORUS: Right on! Right on!

TOP COP: 36 hours on the flat foot
    Got to keep on coming on strong
    Got to push, push, push the hard line
    'Cause I know those freaks are wrong
    Got myself a fancy woman and got myself a Mama copper too
    Got spoilt, ungrateful, mouths to feed
    I gotta do what I gotta do

COP CHORUS: Working overtime
    Working overtime
    We're the thin blue line

The COPS dance forward and attack. A COFFIN BEARER is hit and the tired USHERS drop their burden.

MOZ pops out of the coffin only to find himself staring straight at BANKS, who tries to attack MOZ.

The COPS descend on the pair of them. TREEFROG tries to prevent BANKS being taken but she is beaten back by a cop. They wheel BANKS off to the Black Maria dancing and singing as they go. Other cops grab MOZ and cart him off to the same van.

TREEFROG: I won't leave you!

Singing.

Hold on… I'm coming!

BANKS is wheeled up a ramp and into the van and MOZ is hurled in after him. Before the doors slam shut on the pair of them we see MOZ do a silent Munch-type scream.

ARTHUR comes to, struggles to his knees. TOP COP dances along the red carpet, and towards the dazed ARTHUR. TOP COP rips the number off his uniform, throws it down and raises his baton.

TOP COP: (*Hits ARTHUR.*) Give it to him one time!

The Band hits the beat.

(*Hits* ARTHUR *twice.*) Give it to him two times.

The Band hits two beats.

Three times!

The Band hits three beats.

Get uppa! Get on up! Get uppa! Get on up!

ARTHUR staggers to his feet and TOP COP *beats him down again. Exhausted by the effort,* TOP COP *pretends to faint, James Brown style. Other cops rush forward with a cape and a silk cloth to wipe* TOP COP's *brow. While the* COP *is wiping* TOP COP's *brow he knocks* TOP COP's *wig off. He is completely bald.* TOP COP *raises his baton to strike* ARTHUR *again.*

JENNIFER: Daddy!

TOP COP: (*Looking round flustered. Guiltily tossing baton away.*) Jenny?

JENNIFER runs forward and puts herself between TOP COP *and* ARTHUR.

He attacked me! Poleaxed one of my officers and then came at me like a mad dog.

Pause.

You shouldn't be here…it's dangerous!-

JENNIFER: (*Angry.*) Why is it dangerous?

TOP COP: He was frothing at the mouth…came at me with a…

Looks around for possible weapon, sees only his baton.

Concealed weapon…look it's there!

Points at baton.

He's an outside agitator, shipped in to –

JENNIFER: (*Pointing at baton.*) That's yours.

TOP COP: It was mine…but he took it off me and –

JENNIFER: You're full of bullshit!

JENNIFER picks TOP COP's number up off the floor.

TOP COP: Language lady! I didn't bring you up to use –

JENNIFER: (*Hands him his discarded number.*) This is yours too…

TOP COP: Jennifer… Jenny… I'm your Dad…this is just…
(*Points at ARTHUR.*) Let my lads take care of him; they'll see
that he gets to casualty.

TOP COP motions for the other COPS to pick ARTHUR up.

JENNIFER: (*Helping ARTHUR to his feet.*) Get off him! You're not
touching him! (*To FATHER.*) What are you doing Dad?

TOP COP: It's just work. You may not like it but this what pays
your –

JENNIFER: And you say I'm wasting my life.

TOP COP: Come on Jenny…when you've calmed down well
laugh about this –

Silence.

So I got a bit carried away…my lads have been
hospitalised by these bastards. What do you think that does
to morale? We can't just take it…you can see that? –

Smoking tear gas lands next to them.

JENNIFER: (*Coughing.*) I can't see anything!

*JENNIFER and ARTHUR use the tear gas cover to back away.
Deafening row of klaxons and sirens etc starts up again.*

TOP COP: (*Yelling.*) No more gas, my Daughter's in there…
Jenny, I can get you out of this!

Pause.

Jenny!

TOP COP heads off wrong direction looking for her.

Jenny!

ARTHUR takes his jacket off and gives it JENNIFER.

ARTHUR: Breathe through it.

JENNIFER: What about –

ARTHUR: Take it!

JENNIFER covers her face with the jacket.

TREEFROG runs up to ARTHUR.

TREEFROG: They've got your brother! C'mon!

ARTHUR nods.

TREEFROG runs towards the Black Maria. Everything goes into slow motion.

We're coming…

ARTHUR: (*To JENNIFER as he follows TREEFROG.*) My brother, I've got to…but what's your –

JENNIFER: GO!

TREEFROG gets to Black Maria, puts her hand on the doors, turns around and stops. Action goes back to normal time frame. The Band hit a gospel church chord.

TREEFROG: (*Singing.*) There was year upon year when I felt so alone
When the days were too short and the nights were too long
And I used to pray but it got me nowhere
And so I stopped waiting for him to carry me home

I'm not my Mama's daughter now and you're not your Papa's son
Spent a long time being no one and now I wanna be someone
But it just don't work when you're all alone you never get nothing done

Take my hand, no promised land, common people come
on

I don't believe in Jesus

CHORUS: But she's never on her own

TREEFROG: And if I call?

CHORUS: She knows someone will come

TREEFROG: Will you be beside me

CHORUS: Yeah

TREEFROG: Lord I knew you would

CHORUS: We are the common good

TREEFROG: (*Singing.*) Now god is dead and that's a fact so
amen we're all free
Together we make a mighty wave and you can't hold back
the sea
The times they are a changing and I'm a changing too
Come with me make history, common people come on

I don't believe in Jesus

CHORUS: But she's never on her own

TREEFROG: And if I call?

CHORUS: She knows someone will come

TREEFROG: Will you be beside me

CHORUS: Yeah

TREEFROG: Lord I knew you would

CHORUS: We are the common good

BACK OF BLACK MARIA – CONTINUOUS

In the back of the van BANKS is in his wheelchair. MOZ is on his knees in front of him, BANKS holds MOZ by the hair and has a knife pressing against MOZ's jugular.

BANKS: I'm set in my ways, and I'd miss the human contact. Born 20 years later and I'd switch to the gun but what can you do? We all have our fucking peculiarities.

MOZ: Be a mistake to do it here…back of a police van…just you and me…

BANKS: Enough to send a man spiralling into depression, five years inside, one day out, never even gets to dip his wick and he's back inside. Enough to turn a man suicidal…

MOZ: They'd know it was you, I've got a sister, she wouldn't –

BANKS: Who do you think told us where you were? Your little Sister's going to have terrible guilt when you turn up with your throat slit.

Pause.

She sent us to you, she's gonna wanna forget that…and you. You're a killer, nobody wants you at anniversaries and christenings anymore.

MOZ: It was an accident.

BANKS: Where does it say an eye for an eye unless you poked it out by mistake? My reputation will be worth nowt if I'm seen to be soft wi' you.

Pause.

If it's any consolation this is more necessary than personal.

Pause.

Though I'm not saying it gives me no pleasure.

MOZ: You could just cut me. A little nick or someat, make it look worse than it –

BANKS: Something you should have learnt inside, stab some slag in the leg and he'll spend three months lying on his back working out what he's gonna do to you when he gets back on his feet. Best to do the job right.

The noise of rioting breaks out again outside again. TREEFROG flings open the van doors.

TREEFROG looks at MOZ with his head in BANKS' lap and thinks they are having oral sex.

TREEFROG: Oh dear! Never realised you were… [gay]. Do you want me to come back later?

BANKS: (*Thrusting MOZ away from him.*) No! We're not…it's just… Oh bollocks!

MOZ escapes from the van. He runs for JENNIFER and grabs her hand and drags her off stage. She resists for a moment, looking around for ARTHUR. Unable to see him she lets MOZ drag her away.

TREEFROG runs into the van and grabs BANKS' wheelchair. TREEFROG then runs down the ramp and into the crowd squealing…

TREEFROG: It's like the Great Escape!

BANKS: I had it in hand!

TREEFROG: Don't bother saying thanks!

BANKS: Could have got out on me own.

TREEFROG: Are you always this proud?

BANKS: Yeah.

TREEFROG: Good.

BANKS: Are you always this nosy? And what do you mean good?

Spots ARTHUR.

Where were you sponge brain?

ARTHUR: Are you okay? –

BANKS: Jesus Christ, I was that close to –

Realises that ARTHUR is frantically scanning the crowds.

I'm down here.

ARTHUR: I just met a girl…

BANKS: If she's called frigging Maria don't start singing!

ARTHUR: I don't know where she's gone –

BANKS: The world abounds in twat, and you have to go for one from here…

Pause.

Forget her. We'll get you a nice clean prossie when we get back.

ARTHUR: I don't want a prossie. –

TREEFROG: He doesn't want a prostitute.

Pause.

And you don't either.

BANKS: Never said I did.

TREEFROG: Good.

BANKS: (*Unsettled.*) Good.

Pause.

So you wouldn't like it if I…

TREEFROG: Precisely.

Pause.

I'm doing some street theatre, do you wanna –

BANKS: No.

Pause.

Thanks.

BACK ALLEY – TEN MINUTES LATER

JENNIFER and MOZ run breathlessly into alley – she wears ARTHUR's jacket.

JENNIFER: My Dad's a pig!

MOZ: Your Dad's a pig?

JENNIFER: Don't call him that!

MOZ: You did!

JENNIFER: So…he's my Dad!

Pause.

He was the one in charge of all the cops.

MOZ: Jesus!

JENNIFER: All that crap about law and order… I thought he was like Batman, out there fighting crime.

MOZ: Were you Daddy's little girl then?

JENNIFER: Yeah but I'm not anymore.

MOZ: (*Moving in on her.*) Bet it would piss him off to think of his precious daughter with an ex-con…

JENNIFER: He'd flip.

MOZ: (*Touching her neck.*) That'd show him. (*Nibbling her ears.*) Your ears are warm…

JENNIFER: Someone's talking about me.

MOZ: (*Kissing her neck.*) About how great you look…

JENNIFER: Five years without having a girl.

Slips her hand up his back.

Touch your skin or…

JENNIFER kisses him. All next sets of dialogue is between kisses.

MOZ: All that panic…

JENNIFER: Adrenalin…

MOZ: Fear…did it not make you feel…

JENNIFER: Horny…yeah…all those bodies pressed together, not knowing whether the cops…

MOZ: Your own father…

JENNIFER: Were going to wade in and…

MOZ: You've got long legs… I love long legs… I bet Daddy would freak if he saw them wrapped around…

JENNIFER: You just want to pull a copper's daughter.

MOZ: Correction, I wanna pull the TOP COPPER'S daughter.

JENNIFER starts to unfasten her own trousers with MOZ's help. She tries to struggle out of one trouser leg but it gets stuck on her shoe. MOZ has to help her pull the trouser leg off; the whole operation is ungainly.

MOZ moves towards her.

JENNIFER: Condom!

MOZ starts frantically going through his pockets, finally finding a condom.

MOZ: (*Turning his back on JENNIFER and the audience, trying to put condom on.*) Won't be a minute, I'm getting it… I'm all thumbs, bloody hell…cracked it!

MOZ pulls his pants down and turns back to JENNIFER with his trousers around his ankles and his shirt covering his penis.

JENNIFER tries to hop on to him but he struggles to take her weight and they lurch about awkwardly. His trousers tie his feet together so he can only take small awkward steps.

Is it in?

JENNIFER: Not quite… Bend your knees…

Finally, finally, they achieve penetration.

That's better…

MOZ: (*Moans a couple of times and ejaculates after 20 seconds. Groans.*) I'm sorry…

JENNIFER: What you sorry for?

MOZ stands straight, embarrassed.

MOZ: Ahum.

JENNIFER: What already?

Gets off, embarrassed.

Oh…right. I'd better…

MOZ: Give me a couple of hours I'll be able to go again.

Embarrassed, they start gathering their clothes. MOZ takes the used condom off and is about to drop it on the floor.

JENNIFER: Litter!

MOZ looks around but is unable to find anywhere to put it, sheepishly, he slips the used condom into his pocket.

The Band strikes up a pop tune. JENNIFER and MOZ sing alternate lines. They get dressed as they sing.

(*Singing.*) Could have been so much more.

MOZ: (*Singing.*) Yes! I've done it in the middle of a war!

JENNIFER: (*Singing.*) Could have been the start of something new.

MOZ: (*Singing.*) Yes! Result, I've screwed you!

JENNIFER: (*Singing.*) I don't feel good, I don't feel bad

MOZ: (*Singing.*) Bet I was the best you ever had!

JENNIFER: (*Singing.*) I hope we can still be friends

MOZ: (*Singing.*) Yes! Bagged myself a new girlfriend

Song ends.

JENNIFER: Don't worry about it.

MOZ: I'm not.

Occurs to him to worry.

It's only 'cause it's been a long time.

JENNIFER: There's a technique you can try –

MOZ: I don't need a technique… I can go for hours usually –

JENNIFER: Course you can but it might help if you think of somebody ugly fishing, or unblocking the sink or –

MOZ: I don't need to go fishing!

CELIE appears at the end of the alley.

CELIE: Moz?

Celie runs towards him.

Thank God! Been looking all over for you! Banks turned up after you'd left…he knows you're down here. I've been panicking, thinking if I didn't find you first…

Voice cracking.

And it's all my fault… I'm so sorry.

MOZ: I've seen Banks.

CELIE: And he let you off? Was Jethro with him? I can't find Jethro.

JENNIFER: Who's Banks?

MOZ: (*To JENNIFER.*) You don't want to meet him. (*To CELIE.*) Celie, this is Jennifer.

JENNIFER: We know each other… I've gotta go –

MOZ: But we've just –

CELIE: You saw Banks, what happened when you saw Banks?

JENNIFER: (*To MOZ, trying to escape.*) I'm gonna go find out what's happened to everyone else.

MOZ: I'll come too.

JENNIFER: Stay with your sister...

JENNIFER runs off at speed, giving MOZ no chance to join her.

MOZ: Where will you be?

JENNIFER: Dunno. Maybe catch you later...

MOZ: (*To CELIE.*) You scared her off!

Pause.

How did you get here?

CELIE: Hitched.

MOZ: On your own, at night? You could have ended up on the news!

CELIE: Couldn't just let Banks find you...

MOZ: Thought you didn't care.

CELIE: As if...all that stuff about Dad dying and Mum being ashamed...none of it was... As if she's ashamed, she still thinks the sun shines out of your arse.

MOZ: She'd have been there when I got out if –

CELIE: Even when you were inside, if anybody came round she were still showing off about you, it was all: 'Our David's doing classes now' – she'd just neglect to mention that they were inside Armley jail.

MOZ: You're the college girl.

CELIE: Oh yeah…no matter how many exams I passed, I've never seen her look as pleased as when I gave her that crappy clown that you didn't even paint.

BANKS and ARTHUR appear, each from one side of the stage, cutting off any line of escape.

BANKS: It's a wonderful fucking life is it not, when a man's sister will travel halfway across the country just to watch him die.

Pause.

Bet there's a Johnny Cash song about that.

CELIE: You're not laying a finger on him.

CELIE stands in front of MOZ, shielding him.

Arthur…please…

BANKS: It's not like it is in the films where some arsehole clutches his chest, grunts twice and keels over. Death's a messy business. I should know, watched my sister die…

Points at CELIE.

All things considered, there's symmetry in this.

MOZ steps out from behind CELIE.

MOZ: Go wait at the end for me, I'll be up in a minute. –

BANKS: A fibber right through to the last.

CELIE: I'm not leaving you. I wun't leave you.

MOZ: I know.

Pause.

Go wait for me.

BANKS: Give us a couple of sticks, I need to hobble about shouting: 'And Gawd bless us all'.

CELIE runs at BANKS. BANKS grabs her by the hair and puts a knife to her face.

I'm equal fucking opportunities me.

MOZ: (*Moves towards BANKS, hands up.*) I'm here. Not going anywhere, don't hurt her!

ARTHUR grabs MOZ.

ARTHUR: Like you hurt Kath...

MOZ hunts in his pocket for a weapon, all he can find is the used condom. He hits ARTHUR with it as if it were a cosh. It is absolutely ineffectual.

What the...

Realises it is a used condom.

Ugh! That's disgusting!

ARTHUR chucks MOZ down and lands on top of him. Punching him in the head.

BANKS: There's a knife in your sock!

ARTHUR: I'll use me fists.

Punches MOZ.

Waited a long time for this!

BANKS: Use the knife; we'll be here till last orders.

ARTHUR: Didn't bring it.

MOZ: I don't deserve this.

ARTHUR sits on MOZ and brings his face up to his.

ARTHUR: See me and him?

Jerks head towards BANKS.

Ugly bastards but our Kath weren't ugly, she were beautiful, not just on the outside...made everybody feel special did our Kath…gave you her full attention…and she's not here anymore…'cause of you. Now you're gonna get my full attention.

MOZ: Think I wanted to get into that car?

ARTHUR: Course you did, you were mouthing off.

To BANKS.

Weren't he? –

BANKS: This is all very touching but I want to get to the pub before dark, Arthur, use my knife. –

MOZ: He's a liar! I were pissed when Banks and Kath turned up at that party, she looked so pretty, she'd a mini-skirt and boots and eyes like –

ARTHUR punches MOZ again.

CELIE: Arthur don't hurt him, it wasn't his –

BANKS puts his hand over CELIE's mouth and presses the knife into her face.

BANKS: Shut it! He was trying to chat her up, the randy little git were sniffing round her talking bollocks –

MOZ: I were chatting her up, I were… I liked her, she didn't know how good looking she were and that made her –

BANKS: Leering at her, that's what he were doing!

MOZ: Wasn't like that, I had a crush on her, I were trying to make her laugh and then Banks came up and said he was going –

BANKS: Too right, and I weren't leaving her there with you.

MOZ: He said I had to drive 'em back, told him I was pissed, I'd only passed me test a couple of weeks before. –

BANKS: Dangling your frigging car keys like Sterling Moss. –

MOZ: Banks had a rep, I knew he'd slashed faces.

ARTHUR: So you got behind the wheel.

MOZ: (*Nodding.*) She was in the front.

BANKS: Could see what you were doing in the rear view mirror; there's nowt wrong with my eyes.

MOZ: She were talking and her skirt –

BANKS: Eyes on bastard stalks –

MOZ: Rode up, her skirt rode up and I couldn't help –

BANKS: Trying to see her knickers! –

MOZ: He whacked me on the back of the head –

ARTHUR: With his fist?

MOZ: Something harder…knocked me senseless and –

BANKS: Our Kath went straight through the windscreen 'cause that dirty hound couldn't keep his eyes on the road! –

MOZ: When I came to she was lying on the bonnet, she was too still, wasn't right, her boot had come off… –

BANKS: And that fucker hardly had a mark on him!

MOZ: Her boot was –

ARTHUR: 30 foot up the road. –

MOZ: I didn't even want to get in the car. I should have stood up to him but I didn't…

BANKS: Oh for Christ's sake, be a man, take some responsibility, reminds me of the bloody Germans. (*Whining.*) 'I was just following orders.'

ARTHUR: In the dock, you never said any of this.

MOZ: No-one grasses up Mad Banks…thought it were worth losing five years to keep breathing, didn't realise he was going to kill me anyway.

BANKS: For Christ's sake Arthur, shut him up!

ARTHUR: Give us the knife.

BANKS lets go of CELIE and chucks ARTHUR the knife.

And the bag.

BANKS chucks ARTHUR the bag. ARTHUR pulls out the billy club.

ARTHUR climbs off MOZ, goes towards BANKS with the billy club.

This what you hit him with?

BANKS: Oh Jesus, you don't believe that bollocks do you?

ARTHUR raises the club to strike, stops mid-air, struggling with himself, ARTHUR hurls the club down the alley and begins to walk away.

Where you going?

Points at MOZ.

Look what you've done now! Don't gloat you tosspot! Want a job done, do it your bleeding self!

BANKS jumps out of his chair, runs screaming across the stage on his hands and headbutts MOZ who is still on the floor.

ARTHUR and CELIE run to them. ARTHUR lifts BANKS off MOZ violently and throws BANKS back into his chair.

CELIE hugs MOZ.

ARTHUR: It's not gonna happen, not this time, not ever.

BANKS: But he –

ARTHUR: It was you!

If I thought you'd done it on purpose…

Pause.

All my life I've watched you lash out. Used to think it were because of your legs but you were an evil little sod before you lost 'em.

BANKS: Consistent. That's me.

ARTHUR puts his hands around BANKS throat but instead of throttling him, lifts his hands and touches BANKS' cheeks.

ARTHUR: My big brother, I looked up to you...our sister.

BANKS: I weren't driving!

ARTHUR: You're always driving and I've always been the dickhead sat next to you. I've had enough.

Pause.

You wanna live in a film? Well James Cagney's best mate grassed him up... I've been with you on everything you've done...but it stops now, cause if it doesn't it's gonna all spill out, every pointless piece of shite you've ever done.

BANKS: Fuck yourself up if you did.

ARTHUR: Yeah, cause my life's been one big success up to now.

BANKS: One CSE in woodwork.

Pause.

You can't take a piss without me telling you where to aim.

ARTHUR: So I'll sit down.

BANKS: Without me you'll be just another mongrel.

ARTHUR: Nothing wrong with being a mongrel, carrying a blade doesn't make you a cut above the rest of us, just makes you a little tosser with a knife.

Pause.

Bore somebody else with your gangster bollocks.

BANKS: If it weren't for me you wouldn't be a boxer.

ARTHUR: I'm not a boxer now. –

BANKS: Come on, we're a team, we could be like The Krays.

ARTHUR: One's sad and one's mad. Which one do you want to be?

ARTHUR stands up.

JENNIFER reappears still wearing ARTHUR's coat.

MOZ: Jennifer…

JENNIFER: (*To MOZ.*) You've got my purse… I had to come back for my purse.

ARTHUR: (*To JENNIFER.*) Been looking for you…

JENNIFER: I've still got your coat…

ARTHUR: Keep it, looks better on you.

JENNIFER: No, it looked great on you.

MOZ: Don't mind me, I'm only your boyfriend! –

JENNIFER: You're not my boyfriend!

MOZ: But we… I carried your purse.

JENNIFER: 'Cause I didn't have any pockets!

Pause.

Look we were in a riot, we got carried away but the moment's gone…

MOZ: You're finishing with me? –

JENNIFER: There was never anything to finish.

Pause.

Don't act desperate…it makes you seem –

BANKS: Pathetic. Ah, he's gonna bawl.

MOZ: Shut it!

JENNIFER: Shut it!

Band strikes up 'Yesterday Man' tune.

Music plays quietly under the dialogue still.

MOZ: You're not finishing with me 'cause I'm finishing with you!

JENNIFER: Fine. (*Muttering.*) There's nothing to finish. (*To ARTHUR.*) Where are you going now?

ARTHUR: Back to Leeds.

JENNIFER: Leeds, that's where I'm... I'm Jennifer... Jenny... from Leeds.

ARTHUR holds out his hand to her. They shake hands.

ARTHUR: Arthur, Art. –

JENNIFER: Art. –

BANKS: What's all this art bollocks! –

JENNIFER: I'm an art student. –

BANKS: Oh Jesus it gets worse!

Pause.

He's a piss artist!

JENNIFER: Do you want a lift back up to Leeds in the van; I'm sure there'll be room. –

BANKS: Nah, we're hitching. –

ARTHUR: That would be great.

JENNIFER and ARTHUR start to leave.

BANKS: Where you going?

ARTHUR: (*Turning.*) Home. (*Making a decision, to JENNIFER.*) He's a giant pain in the arse but he's my brother...

JENNIFER: He could go in the back, well be up front.

ARTHUR: (*To BANKS.*) If you come you've got to behave yourself.

BANKS: No thanks, I'll make alternative arrangements, I'm too old to be on reins.

ARTHUR: Please yourself. I asked.

JENNIFER: (*To MOZ.*) What about you two… If you're stuck we could –

CELIE: Forget it. We'll get the coach, wouldn't want my brother cramping your style – there might be a bloke in that van you haven't had.

JENNIFER: (*Leaving.*) He's a big boy now, doesn't need you to look after him.

JENNIFER and ARTHUR leave.

MOZ: I do, I do need you to look after me.

CELIE: I know. C'mon, let's go see Mum.

Pause.

Told you not to get off with her.

CELIE and MOZ begin to leave.

(*Turning to BANKS.*) My boyfriend Jethro, he set off with you.

BANKS: Last seen in Beeston with that scrap heap of a car.

CELIE: Did you…

BANKS: (*Holds his hands up.*) Never even hurt his feelings.

Spotlight lights up the car at the side of the stage. JETHRO and RICHARD the balloon salesman are inside it. The car is full of balloons and JETHRO is frantically blowing up more.

RICHARD: Bigger…oooh that's so big!

The spotlight goes out again.

CELIE: (*To BANKS.*) Will you be alright?

BANKS: Don't you start!

Points off stage.

Hell be lost without me, lost!

CELIE and MOZ leave.

BANKS sits alone on stage in his wheelchair. He wheels it around a little, at a loss for what to do.

(*Shouting.*) Don't start thinking I'll crack and follow you cause I won't…I'm alright me, I'm fine, better than fine, brilliant, that's what I am, brilliant…

Gets hip flask out and toasts.

Top of the world Mama! Top of The World!

Drinks last dregs. Chucks empty flask away. Wheels himself around the stage.

Could go anywhere, do anything. You've not eliminated my options mate!

Shouts.

She's cunt-washed you, it's like brainwashing but it smells worse!

TREEFROG appears.

TREEFROG: Do you always have such a dirty mouth on you?

BANKS: Yeah.

TREEFROG: Good.

BANKS: Just got rid of me brother.

TREEFROG: Have you?

BANKS: I'm not a baby sitter. –

TREEFROG: I've just seen him.

Pause.

He asked me to give you a lift. –

BANKS: I don't want charity.

TREEFROG: Good.

BANKS: Why's that good?

TREEFROG: I've got a cat. I don't need another tame pet.

BANKS: What do you want?

TREEFROG: Don't know yet; I'll think about it on the way back up.

BANKS: I never said I'd come.

TREEFROG: Good.

Pause.

Wouldn't want you if you came too easily.

BANKS: Bit forward for a hippy.

TREEFROG: I'm a complicated hippy.

BANKS: If I let you give me a lift it doesn't mean…

TREEFROG: Worried that I'll take advantage of you?

BANKS: Your name's Treefrog, as if you could get the upper hand.

TREEFROG: And if my name was Elli, short for Eileen?

BANKS: Elle's better, like a French bird.

TREEFROG: Elle, Elle's good.

Pause.

Something old, something new…

BANKS: We're not getting frigging married.

Pause.

We don't match, look at your trousers.

TREEFROG: We can go shopping.

Pause.

You can get new trousers.

The End.

Thanks to:

- *Lee Dalley at Leeds University for the use of the Workshop Theatre for rehearsals*

- *Diana Tyler – MBA Literary Agents*

- *Stephen Watson – Oberon Books*

- *Dawn Wilkinson – Yorkshire Dance*

- *Andy Wood – Q Division*

- *Ben Eaton & Victoria Pratt for video footage.*

- *Staff at Northern Ballet Workshop*